Instead of Veto

A Revolutionary UN Vision for the Survival of Mankind

Written by Tibor Magyar

New Generation Publishing

CONTENTS

Foreword

Dear Reader,

The veto system in the United Nations (UN) Security Council's decision-making on security issues is obviously a sensitive problem, because the invited experts did not give any opinion for this book. Their silence is loud. Either their selection was wrong or they did not want to support a "nobody" in their field.

They obviously might think that the veto system is a necessary wrong issue, instead of which famous politicians and acknowledged experts have not been able to offer a better solution since the creation of the UN. Therefore the solution is a kind of social version of a perpetual motion machine, which does not exist. It could have been right if the examination of circumstances had not been able to step out of the earlier examination spectrum. The spectrum has been extended and so many new inventions have emerged this way. Sometimes, "nobodies" have discovered them. Now, technological revolution opens new highways for speeding up qualitative social development.

Please give credit in advance and at least one or two hours of your time to read this book, which was prepared with the intention of saving you and your families' lives, and judge yourself whether it was worth it or not. Sorry for the big words!

Preface

Studying the updated annual report of the Global Challenges Foundation (GFC)[1] it could be concluded that two things can save mankind from catastrophic risks, a quick technological and a social revolution. These are mutually interrelated. If one of them is behind or not fast enough then humanity has no chance of survival. Only effective world governance could be able to coordinate mandatory qualitative changes. Therefore a revolutionary UN reform is crucial.

Although the conclusion could demand scientific proof and after that it still could be discussed it can be stated that the current UN system seems to be too bureaucratic and ineffective. It seems to be so especially for a military who has worked in different national and international joint staffs, where everything has been coordinated and organized in space and time for mission accomplishment. Therefore, a military perspective might be interesting for civilians on the necessary changes in the UN and its problem solution system.

This essay is a modified and supplemented model description, which was created based on the application material, under the title of "Suggestions to the modernization of the world governance". It was submitted on New Shape Prize 2018 competition, initiated by the GCF. Hopefully, the current modified version will be more understandable for readers thanks to the absence of word and image limitation.

This vision is not intended to be either a utopia or a collection of average solutions. On the one hand it is suggested to be food for thought, which might be useful for experts accomplishing the planned "profound change"[2] in the UN. On the other hand, this is a kind of attempt to draw people's attention to unavoidable changes in the society.

The model description was made by theoretical system approach, based on the reports of GFC on global challenges and personal research and experience, which were collected during almost a decade long work as a national military force planner in the Hungarian Defence Forces, cooperating with NATO and EU planners.

---

1 Global catastrophic risks. Internet, https://api.globalchallenges.org/static/files/GCF-Annual-report-2018-BW.pdf
2 In: Secretary-General's remarks on the Second Report on the Repositioning of the UN Development System. Internet, https://www.un.org/sg/en/content/sg/statement/2018-01-22/secretary-generals-remarks-second-report-repositioning-un

Introduction

So far, human development has been accompanied with a series of armed conflicts. Why is it so? Is it, because unequal development could not exist in human societies durably? For that, the fall of the Roman Empire could be a yes answer, when less developed nations toppled down the developed part of the world.

Theoretically, the world without conflicts requires nations somewhere on the same level of development.

In order to sweep traditional contradictions under the carpet between nations and different cultures and provide the necessary development, there have been some direct globalization attempts. For example: in the case of the Warsaw Pact countries, where an artificial social system wanted to keep nations behind a "protected" iron curtain, or the NATO mission in Afghanistan where the military and civilians got together for the stabilization of the country. They intended to export some development, especially in the area of infrastructure.

Until now, these direct attempts have not been very successful, because different nations and cultures are hardly willing to accept sudden and/or enforced changes.

In the mean time, looking at ecological footprint calculations, it is easily recognizable that the traditional way of raising developing countries to the level of developed countries is almost impossible on the current technology level, because it would need the space equivalent to more Earth-type planets.

If the statement is true, the artificial mixture of nations and cultures seems to be problematic, because this way human society could drop to a lower standard. It could not be acceptable to those who experienced a higher standard.

So far, more or less, nations developed separately and there was always a big war, which established a kind of new order between nations for supremacy according to the evolving power structure. Now, if another world war were to happen, it could destroy not only humanity, but all life on planet Earth.

1. The UN reform is indispensable

1.1. Changes in the security environment

To prevent international conflicts and promote international cooperation, an intergovernmental organization, the UN was created in the wake of World War II by the victorious powers.

The Preamble of the UN Charter says: "Peoples of the UN are determined to save succeeding generations from the scourge of war."

Ever since the creation of the UN, the world power structure has changed significantly. For example: the bipolar world order changed into one polar, a bit later multi-polar. New financial and economic centers have emerged mainly in Asia.

New nuclear powers have been created. The European Union has been established.[3] Next to the integration there was a disintegration process, which was rarely peaceful (like in Yugoslavia). Structural changes often caused social changes (as the Arab Spring). The terrorism and religious radicalism has become a worldwide challenge.

The UN institutions, especially the decision-making system has not been able to follow all the changes. This way the world governance cannot exclude possible contradictions of interest in decision-making between ruling powers and real world power structure, which can lead to a veto frequently in the UN Security Council.

How to continue? Would it be possible to establish a conflict-free world that exists on a lower level of development and/or would it be worth it to risk an apocalypse anyway?

None of these are realistically possible. How do we get through major problems in human society and change the bigger fish practice in the future?

Finding the answers quickly is much more immense than ever before, because besides the potential armed apocalypse mankind is creating more and more **global challenges, which can cause irreversible damage to nature.**

The interdependent character of these challenges is getting obvious and the world governance cannot be effectively operated by disintegrated and fragmented organizations which the UN currently has.[4]

Because of the aforementioned features the UN has to make tremendous efforts to coordinate different strategic planning cycles of different subject areas and the work of their autonomous organizations.

From the UN Headquarters only one is located in a developing part of the world (in Nairobi, Kenya). All the fifteen specialized UN agencies are located in developed areas. Developing countries, as major consumers of the UN programs are usually far from the place where their requests are judged.

The bureaucratic UN organizations are exposed to the wavering budget sources. Sometimes, the abuse of power also exists.

Nevertheless, the biggest problem is the inefficiency in decision-making.

The veto rule in the UN Security Council may paralyze the problem solution. Usually, small nations are victim of that, because the necessary actions are often delayed. For example: the massacre in Srebrenica, in 1995, during the Yugoslavian war.

There were not too many successes in the proliferation of weapons of mass destruction (WMD).

---

3 Jean Claude Juncker stated in his State of the union 2018 speech: The European Union has to reach the ability of world politics ("Weltpolitik fähigkeit"). In: EU press release data base, Strasbourg 12 Sep 2018.
4 The UN include the affiliated programs, funds and specialized agencies all with their membership, leadership and budget and different planning systems.

There is also room for criticism in the area of fair trading regulations.

The "America first" point of view that is spreading all over the world is nothing to be admired. Nevertheless, it may lead to more separation and less cooperation of nations and more conflicts.

Now, world powers of different levels spin their limits and try to expand for energy resources or line of communications geographically (the Arctic, Chinese Sea, in Syria and so on) or in the new dimension as the cyber space and social influences in their strategic game. For the reason that big players have considerably strong nuclear capacity, beside the routine economic blockade or trading sanction and financial restrictions and diplomatic frictions the prevention and the cost efficiency of maintaining traditional operations have become the special viewpoints. Small players started to dream about a bigger role in the shadow of powers. Nothing to be sure, only that the number of civilian casualties and the fleeing migrants and refugees is getting higher.

The first served first based rule is about to change the existing world order, and it states that effective world governance is still missing and it is very dangerous for all people.

In the interest of handling global challenges successfully it is a must to establish more effective world governance, which can strengthen sustainable development by social and technological modernization and coordinate sub-regional, regional cooperation promoting gradual integration of nations.

There is no need to risk a catastrophic failure and no time to establish a new world order. Hopefully, the current world leaders and their governments recognize the necessity of the UN reform in order to insure the survival of the Earth's biosphere and within it, humanity itself.

It should be outlined that there will not be enough to protect the environment; the whole human society should be changed. Inside of it, the international decision-making mechanism is the most important to be turned from the language of strength into the language of sustainability and integration.

Hopefully, the world leaders can understand that to be strong is not enough and they must be modern too. They should be aware of that the traditional power components of society like armed forces or the extensive economy or financial power and their use against less strong nations serves as the deterrence of potentially strong enemies, which can make temporary alliances only. They should recognize that **sustainability and integration as possible new power components may serve the collective survival of humanity** and attract enduring alliances from mutual interest. Therefore, the world governance should promote that the **force-based power components of the society could be gradually shrunk and turned into the subject of a balanced competition in the area of the sustainability and integration.**

Although, the traditional force based power components should be acknowledged still for a long time, **the new power components should be welcomed on getting higher level.**

It will not contradict the colorfulness of cultures of different nations and their specific way of thinking.

1.2. The scope of the reform

A new unified evaluation system, which prefers the sustainable development and integration, should be introduced. The UN organizations should be functionally and hierarchically restructured according to the global challenges and handling of their regional and sub-regional necessities. The UN Charter needs to be renewed for current and future development. The UN Security Council's composition should be changed according to the changing world power structure and the results in the competition of sustainable development and integration. The traditional power based votes in the UN Security Council, need to be qualified on sustainability and integration.

The UN proactive crisis management capabilities must be developed. The UN strategic planning system should be integrated and coordinated in the same planning cycle. The self-sustainability of the UN must be established.

1.3. The end state

The **UN decision-making and problem solution system could promote sustainable development and integration effectively.** This way, human civilization could step into a new generation.

2. New evaluation system

In different subject areas, the UN has different evaluation systems for showing development. **A unified evaluation system of the sustainable development and integration** introduced for the UN member states' governments **could be a good tool** for the initiation of the modernization. Nevertheless, traditional force-based power components should be acknowledged still and they need to be evaluated.

The system of different subject criteria should be elaborated by the UN councils and their organizations. Their results should be coordinated with national experts. During the coordination, UN experts need to pursue for the acknowledgement of traditional power components could lose their significance.

They need to reach that, before a new evaluation cycle starts, an internationally accepted evaluation system was created in accordance with the new sustainability and integration goals. If necessary, the UN functional structure should be harmonized with the composition of new evaluation criteria.

Next to the traditional subject areas, national governments should be evaluated on every new subject, in which they accept sustainable development and integration goals. They should be pushed to collecting getting more evaluation points. Some priority areas (the proliferation of WMD or human rights, for example) could be suggested to a government and **special bonus points should be available** to them for the accomplishment. It should be considered that national governments could be provided with **positive discrimination points based upon their own judgment too**, on those areas, where the results they deem important and usable for the whole world community.

2.1. Theoretical base for criteria

The democratic political system and the acceptance of human rights are characteristic for a progressive government.

It should be appreciated, if a government operates a transparent and accountable institutional system. The less a nation state suppresses its citizens the more positive the evaluation. Compliance with international law is indispensable for a durable peaceful existence.

If the government's projects are in harmony with long term sustainable goals and available resources then it should be acknowledged. Financial stability should be welcomed.

If a government looks to the military and the police as final guarantors of peace and security then their capabilities and professional values should be acknowledged. If a government offers deployable forces enabling UN for quick reaction, it should be welcomed. In contrast, a government should not strive to obtain WMD; rather it is more favorable to put the wellbeing of its people above all else.

It shall be accounted as very negative if a government cannot control radical paramilitary organizations or even worse, if it supports terrorist groups.

A government should be rewarded if it invests in health and biosphere protection, environmentally friendly technologies, and supports the consumption of alternative energy resources.

The establishment of fossil-based power stations should be avoided if possible.

Regarding nuclear power stations; reliable security measures and control systems should be supported, but examination of whether a power station replaces fossil-based stations or not is required.

The cultural values of nations should be supported by governments. The glory of their history and tradition, the beauty of their language, the cohesive strength of their religion, the excellence of their education and science, the performance of their artists and sportsmen/sportswomen worthily expect appreciation. However, religious radicalism also exists, which has a very negative effect on development. If a government does not make differences between religion and state it may result in unfair discrimination.

It is more beneficial if the government's projects are coordinated with other states and non-governmental organizations. It should be acknowledged if a government recognizes that regional cooperation is more favorable than bilateral. This way developing nations will close the gap between them and developed nations, and developed nations will become safer. So, this is a mutual interest. The global integration can be a precondition to persistent survival of nations. In accordance with this assumption we may not be happy with any willingness of disintegration. Nevertheless, it would be a mistake if a regional or a global power intended to integrate a nation by force. This could deepen the existing identity dissimilarities and delay global integration. Therefore, it should be assessed as positive if a government gives the requested right of cultural or territorial autonomy to minorities. Presumably, the easier the autonomy was given the more temporary the disintegrated period. It should be considered positive as well, if two nations separate peacefully and establish new states. The support of developing areas in the interest of their convergence should be acknowledged properly. Contribution to peace operations, humanitarian aid, and the assistance in the operation of a refugee camp or the reception of refugees should be appreciated on a high level. However, if refugees arrive illegally and cause unjustified chaos in developed regions, they run the risk of ruining the civilians' willingness in their support. Consequently, the registration and interception efforts should be understood.

2.2. New method of the evaluation

2.2.1. How to prefer sustainability as a power component

Although there are some new methodologies[5], the current development is still usually internationally measured by Gross Domestic Product (GDP). GDP comes at expense of human and material resources. Resource production needs energy. So, the quantity of energy consumption could be examined in relationship with measuring development. For sustainability to be preferred in human development, a kind of new, **"sustainable GDP" (SGDP)** should be expressed from energy consumption, examining **how much of its part originates from alternative energy sources**, or it could be even better to take only its renewable part (without the performance of nuclear power stations).

Environmental protection and rehabilitation should receive positive discrimination, so the part of the GDP, which was allocated to that, could be perceived as part of SGDP and it could be added to the calculation.

Different subject areas should be evaluated by the responsible UN organizations based on their own elaborated evaluation system.

In order to different subject values could be summarized, the average values should be calculated. After that, positive or negative value points should be given, depending on the difference from **the average** on a scale up or down. This way relative value points could be obtained.

The average calculation could be similar to the competence measurement applied in school classes, where student performances are compared to each other.

The average calculation and the subsidizing systems on the actual outcome of the evaluation could support that the unequal development of nations was balanced permanently.

---

[5] For example: Physical Quality of Life Index (PQLI), Human Development Index (HID), and Quality of Life Index (QLI).

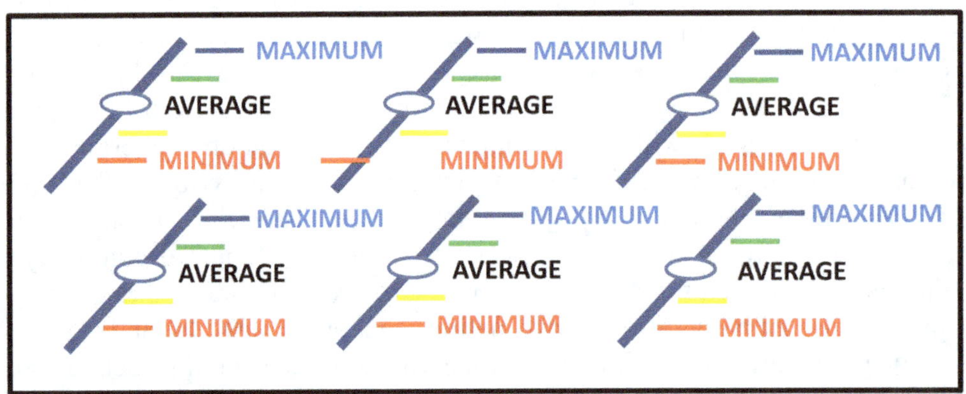

In the following, relative value points should be compared with SGDP. This way, SGDP could be a qualifier.[6]

2.2.2. How to unify and prefer integration as a power component

The relative subject values could be unified by the means of the adaptation of military quality power relations, where the level of the integration could be a qualifier.

Different qualifying coefficients and values could be applied:

"Y" (yellow), "G" (green), "B" (blue) coefficient; multiplies a relative subject value depending on its sub-regional, or regional or global importance[7];

"U"- unifying coefficient; multiplies the sum of a relative subject value depending on its importance in the comparison of other subject areas;

"R" (red), "Y" (yellow), "G" (green), "B" (blue) values; values of national, sub-regional, regional and global importance;

"Unified" value; the unified value of a subject area.

---

[6] In the suggested methodology the UN experts always measure development in a subject area based on their own methodology. If a new other than GDP method was internationally introduced, the new measurement should be compared with the preferred alternative energy production ratio.

[7] Large sustainable countries could be perceived as regional powers, so their governments' activities could be multiplied by regional qualifying coefficients.

THE UNIFIED EVALUATION SYSTEM

Sustainable development and integration								
			Criteria and standards and „Y" / „ G" / „B" /"Unifying" coefficient explanatory					
Subject areas	Subject groups	Subject branches	„R" value	„Y" value	„G" value	„B" value	Sum	Unified value
			Evaluation					
	Value points obtained by a government							
	Textual evaluation of a government							

An example is shown for the calculation:

As a traditional power component, a nation state-owned WMD gives a relative basic value. If this was offered to the UN (it would be under UN arms-control) then it could have global importance, because it could be part of an integrated global defense system; In this case we need to multiply it by the blue coefficient.

If just a part of the WMD was offered to the UN and another part to NATO, then the first would get a global (blue) and the second a regional (green) qualifier.

Next, we need to add this value to other military capabilities.

Depending on the importance of the military, we multiply the military capabilities by a unified coefficient and finally we obtain the qualified relative value, which can be added to other qualified relative values of subject areas.

The methodology could be adapted in any subject area. In economy area, for example, if a new electric power line integrates the electricity supply of a sub-region, the evaluation should be multiplied by "yellow coefficient" for the cooperating governments. If a special good production, for example, certain number of commercial airplane was produced in regional cooperation, than it should be accounted by "green coefficient". In trade area, regional free trading activities could be accounted by regional coefficient. In cultural area, if two countries take part with a common team in the Olympic game, their result should be accounted by sub-regional coefficient.

In health protection area, physician teams' activities in one of the UN humanitarian actions could get global coefficient. In environment rehabilitation area, participation in a future geoengineering activity could be acknowledged by global coefficient too.

2.2.3. The evaluating algorithm and its formulas

The calculation of SGDP Power Component (SGDP PC)
1. The UN experts should use their own methodology and prepare their evaluation in a subject ($E_{UN\ EXP}$)
2. The average result of the governments ($A_{UN\ EXP}$) should be shown
3. Relative value points of a government (RVP_{GOV}) should be calculated

4. The Sustainable GDP (the percentage of GDP, which was obtained by renewable energy and which was allocated to environmental protection and rehabilitation -$SGDP_{GOV}$) should be expressed
5. Relative value points should be multiplied with SGDP/100 (RVP_{GOV} X $SGDP_{GOV}$/100)

The calculation of Integration Level Power Component (IL PC)
6. The Coefficient of Integration Level (sub-regional or regional or global)- (COE_{INTL}) should be obtained
7. Integration Level Power Component should be calculated (SGDP Power Component should be multiplied with the Coefficient of Integration Level- SGDP PC X COE_{INTL})

The calculation of unified value points
8. The Unifying Coefficient (COE_{UN}) of a subject area should be obtained
9. The unified value points (UVP_{GOV}) should be calculated (SGDP Power Component should be multiplied with Unifying Coefficient-SGDP PC X COE_{UN})
10. The unified value points should be summarized

Remark: If a relative value is negative than it should be multiplied with 100-SGDP percentage or 10-COE_{INTL} if COE_{INTL} not greater than 10, instead of shown above in the formulas, otherwise the evaluation will not be correct. If the subject of evaluation is a negative thing, such as supporting sub-regional or regional level terrorist groups or breaching diplomatic immunity of state's or state union's diplomats the COE_{INTL} should remain as was shown in the formulas. So, it could increase the negative value.

2.3. The use of the evaluation in practice

Applying the demonstrated evaluating algorithm and its formulas, the UN experts could compose **a new ranking list of national governments' performance**.

The list and the textual evaluations could be issued every second year temporarily and every ten years permanently, closing an evaluation cycle.

If a government's subject area is below the standard minimum the effective usage of available resources should be examined.

The result can help to decide whether a government should be supported or/and provided with suggestions for improvements. **This way, the sustainable development competition will be balanced and those developing nations, which were temporarily left behind, will be pushed to reach the level of developed.**

National governments could be systematically inspected and depending on a possible shortfall, they could be warned. Sanction necessities should be negotiated by the UN Security Council. The Security Council's decision may have influence on the government's convergence funds next year, which could be reduced or suspended until the shortfall was amended. Nevertheless, a new government would be eligible to access all its convergence funds. This way people could see the government was wrong and not the nation.

3. Functional restructuring

In order to meet the requirements of the world's global challenges, the governance's functional areas should be restructured. Because of the interdependence of global challenges, the world governance should be functionally coordinated.

The bases of the sustainable development of the society are **peace and stability**; therefore the connecting functions should be coordinated and operated accordingly. **Health and environmental protection and cultural values** could also be connected. From the crisis prevention point of view, distinguished attention should be devoted to **international cooperation** and **minority protection**. High priority should be given to the coordination of **refugee and migrant management**.

FUNCTIONAL RESTRUCTURING

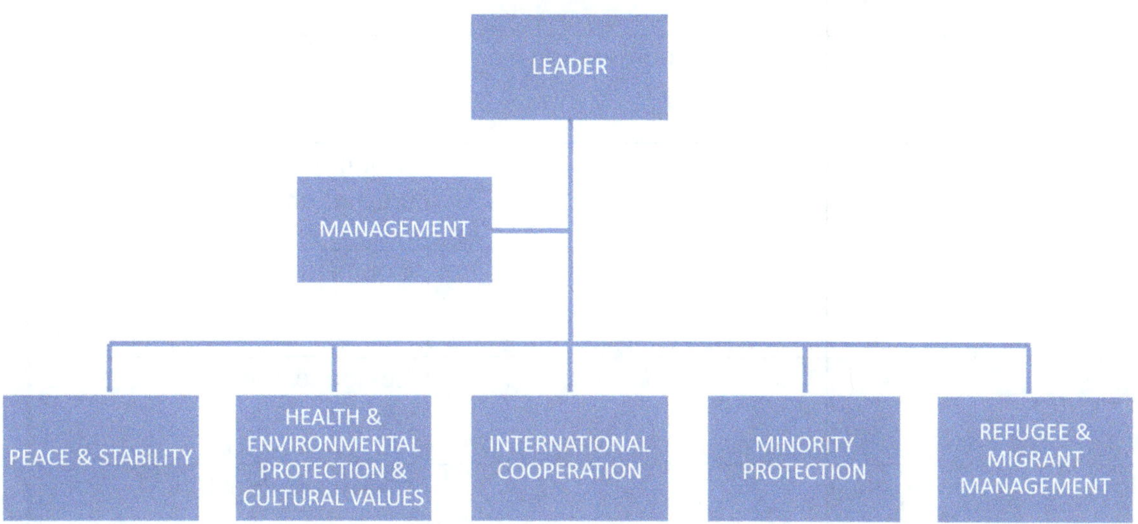

For the proper coordination of functional areas **the new functions need to be supported by a coordinator body**. That is why the management's function should consist of the **planning coordination**. That way the restructuring could be controlled properly as well. Every functional block should be connected to the management by **liaison subject matter experts (LSMEs)**.

The composition of functional elements shown in the next table intended to mirror a theoretical approach, is obviously not complete and can be subject to changes in accordance with the actual structure of sustainability and integration goals of the UN. The demonstrated composition was created based on a concept in accordance with "the theoretical base for criteria" in the chapter 2.1.

Based on the numbered blocks council level organizations could be established.

The functions listed in the second column of the chart could require a department; in the third column a branch or an office size supporting staff organization.

A NEW FUNCTIONAL COMPOSITION (THEORETICAL VERSION)

subject areas	subject groups	subject branches
Management of the sustainable development (1. block)	Development planning	Policy
		Restructuring

	Human management	Staff resources
		Staff material drivers
	Planning Coordination	Feasibility
		Monitoring and anti corruption
		Complaints
		Lesson learned
		LSMEs (2. block)
		LSMEs (3. block)
		LSMEs (4. block)
		LSMEs (5. block)
		LSMEs (6. block)
	Current affairs	Administration
		Official duties
		Security
		Peace operations
		Assembly/conference management

		Media

	Trusteeship representation	Peace and stability
		Environmental and health protection and cultural values
		International cooperation
		Minority protection
		Refugee and migrant management
	Third sector interface (Non-governmental representation)	Advisers
		Private supporters
		Associations, movements
		Foundations
Peace and stability (2. block)	Planning coordination	LSMEs (3. block)
		LSMEs (4. block)
		LSMEs (5. block)

		LSMEs (6. block)

	Stability of political system	Democratic values
		Social system
	Human rights	Right to the life
		Right of freedom
		Right to work
		Race equality
		Gender equality
		Child protection
	International law	Law of nations
		Agreements between nations
	Sustainable economic development	Industry

		Agriculture
		Trade
		Transportation
		Telecommunication
		Research and development
	Resources	Human resources
		Fossil resources and their technology modernization
		Alternate resources
		Mining and mineral exploitation
	Financial stability	Financial institutions
		Financial markets
		Credit environment
	Military and police capabilities	WMD
		High-tech weapon systems
		Conventional systems

| | | Police |
| | | Antiterrorism |

Environmental and health protection and cultural values (3. block)	Planning coordination	LSMEs (2. block)
		LSMEs (4. block)
		LSMEs (5. block)
		LSMEs (6. block)
	Environmental Protection	Biosphere protection
		Climate changes prevention
		Fossil energy reduction
		Renewable energy increase
		Recycling, recultivation, water and air purification
	Population control	Motivations and regulations
		Information

	Health protection	Health preservation, illness prevention
		Treatment
		Rehabilitation
	Cultural values	Education
		Language
		Science
		Art
		Religion
		Tradition and treasure protection
		Tourism
		Sport
International Cooperation (4. block)	Planning coordination	LSMEs (2. block)
		LSMEs (3. block)
		LSMEs (5. block)
		LSMEs (6. block)

	Sub-regional/regional/ global cooperation	Security cooperation
		Economic cooperation, development programs, trading accords
		Infrastructural cooperation
		Environmental cooperation
		Cultural cooperation
Minority protection (5. block)	Planning coordination	LSMEs (2. block)
		LSMEs (3. block)
		LSMEs (4. block)
		LSMEs (6. block)
	Traditional minority	General political rights
		Cultural autonomy
		Territorial autonomy
	Adopted people	Accommodation and job opportunities
		Education and freedom of culture

		Orphan trusteeship

Refugee and migrant management (6. block)	Planning coordination	LSMEs (2. block)
		LSMEs (3. block)
		LSMEs (4. block)
		LSMEs (5. block)
	Camp establishment and operation	In home area
		Out of home area
	Camp support	Financial support
		Human and material support
	Movement management	Registration and reception
		Interception of illegally moving people
		Administrative procedures, relocation

4. Hierarchical restructuring

In order to achieve the sustainable and integration goals as quickly as possible the reform should be implemented not only in the UN high level organizations, but on lower and middle level, namely on people, companies and banks, foundations and their supporters' level.

4.1. Lower level

In the UN framework a global sustainable development movement, **for example the UN Blue Planet Movement (UNBPM)** should be initiated. People should be encouraged to contribute to environmental protection and consume environmentally friendly products which can be supported by the UNBPM. If people send an invoice copy to a UNBPM center they would be eligible for reimbursement. **Reimbursements** can be financed from companies' promotions and people's contributions. The UNBPM should offer different possibilities to contribute to in the form of **supporting tickets**. For example: clean energy, clean water, rainforest, poverty, child protection, animal protection, bio food. The supported products should be grouped and financed in accordance with the structure of tickets. In order to inspire people's contribution, the UNBPM should select winners at random for travel, cultural, educational, communication service package etc. By buying the products signed with the UNBPM trademark, people sooner or later could be separated from the central, still generally fossil-based energy network, and could reduce their energy consumption. Nation states should not impose higher tax to UNBPM supported products. Furthermore, they should guarantee that people could get their reimbursement.

4.1.1. One Star Level UNBPM membership requirements

One Star Level members could be requested for a UN vote on the Internet in order to be convinced about people's opinion on a subject. Everybody can be a One Star Level member, who registered and declared that he or she acknowledges UNBPM environmental and social co-existential friendly principles:

"I undertake that I live in accordance with UNBPM environmental and social co-existential friendly principles. If I have the possibility I will buy the UNBPM supported products and I am aware of the fact that this way I contribute to sustainable development. If possible, I use solar, wind, water, ground or other renewable energy resources. I will do anything I can for the reduction of fossil based energy consumption. I support and I conduct selective trash collection, if possible.

I deliver dangerous materials and sewage coming from my household into designated storage. I do not solve my problems by force. I refrain from any physical or mental force and I withdraw myself from any activities which could lead to an addiction, like drugs or unreasonable alcohol consumption. I take care of the health of myself and others. I stop my activities if they disturb people. I do not take part in any terrorist group's activity and I do not support it. If I am informed about a terrorist activity I report it to the officials immediately."

4.1.2. Two Star Level UNBPM membership requirements

A One Star Level member could be a Two Star Level member if he or she can prove a clean life record and successfully complete a basic level knowledge test uploaded to the Internet about UN principles. The reason for that is, **Two Star Level members could be addressed for an official UN decisive vote on the Internet.**

After taking the exam they need to take an oath:

"Hereby I swear that the copy of my clean life record, which I sent to the UNBPM, is a copy of a valid document issued by an official authority. I declare that I agree with UN principles written in the UN Charter. Furthermore, I swear that before UN votes I will have thoughtfully studied all UN campaign materials uploaded to the Internet and I will not leave anybody to sway my judgment."

4.1.3. The logo of the UNBPM

Nine points in a frame of a quadrate can be connected with four straight lines if the drawer went outside of the frame. It refers to the outer majority because the majority of voting people will be out of the region where the problem exists. Thus, the UNBPM members represent a qualified outer majority, because they are able to represent not only their own interest but the others' too.

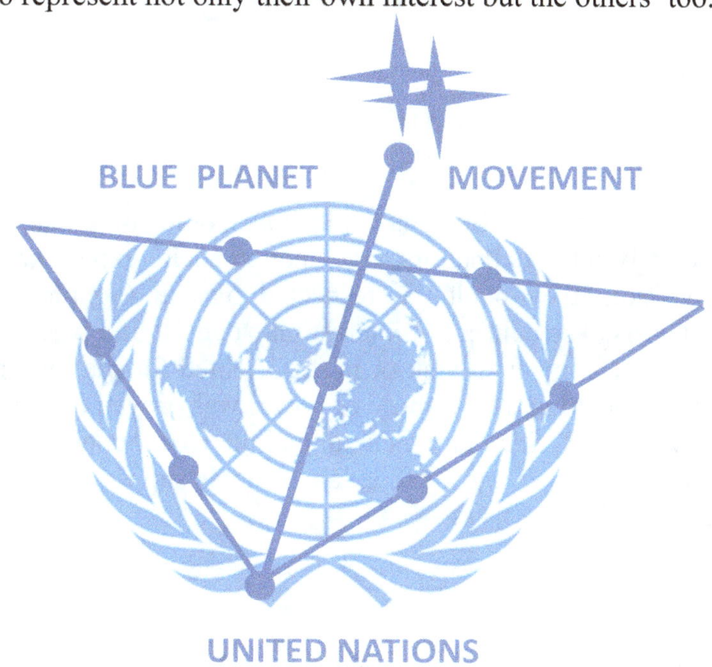

4.2. Medium level

The **UNBPM offices publicizing UN principles should be established in big cities** and they could work together with mayor's offices, **national UN associations** and civilian organizations. Agreement must be reached about that companies and banks pay a small part of their **corporate tax to the UN (UN tax)**. The tax can be reimbursed if the profit was acquired from environmentally friendly production and invested in developing areas and partially reimbursed if it was invested elsewhere. From the tax the UN could generate funds to convergence programs and humanitarian aids and issue tenders for the companies and banks to invent environmentally friendly technologies. Beyond this, the tax can help finance the extra cost of UN restructuring. **Private entities and companies and banks' owners could be multistage level voluntary supporters of the UN.**

Support of nonprofit UN related foundations' activities should be acknowledged as well.

Depending on the amount and the importance of the contribution, supporters could reach One Star (national) Two Star (sub-regional) Three Star (regional) Four Star (global) Levels.

From the UN supporters the UN Secretary General could nominate councilors to the UN Assembly for acceptance. If wealthy councilors have enough social experience and their interest does not conflict with the position, they could be respected official (country, sub-regional, regional, global) UN mediators, advisers. The conflict of interest may consist of a party membership, member in leadership or ownership in any company, bank or profit-oriented foundation or religious organization in the area of authority of the position. If the abuse of power was proved the councilor should be called back by the UN Assembly. The UN Secretary General and the UN councilors have the right to request UNBPM members to vote in order to know the extent of their support to a solution and represent a stronger position during mediation.

4.3. High level

In the interest of a more effective integration support, the hierarchy of global governance should be reestablished from the current fragmented structure into a characteristically more consumer friendly, joint environment.

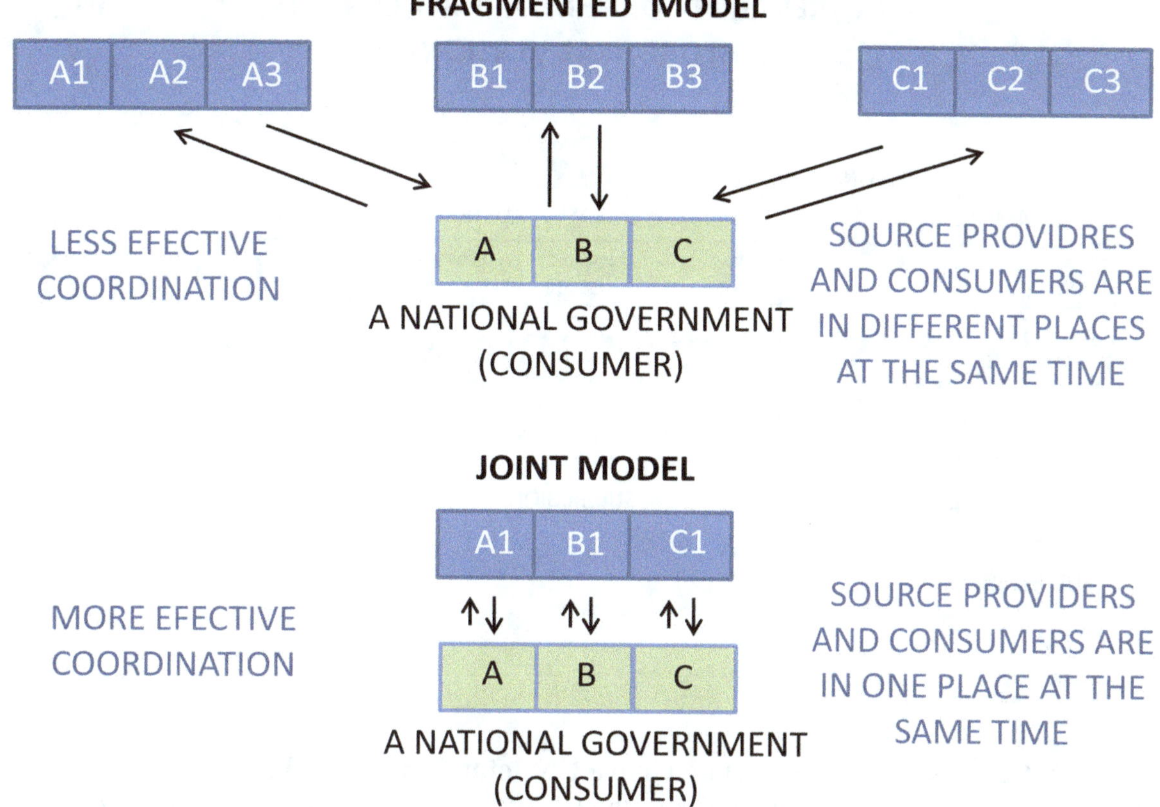

The UN organizations should inspire national governments for the development of their system being able to be integrated into sub-regional or regional or global governance. A common identity source could be found and emphasized in every geographically connecting area. **A new common identity could neutralize a stubborn national interest.** Therefore, where deemed necessary (for example: in Central America, South America (perhaps more) and East Europe, South Europe and Nord Africa, Central Africa, South Africa and the Middle East and Central Asia, South East Asia, and the Pacific) a **UN Joint Sub-regional Center (UNJSC)** should be established.

The centers should coordinate the planning and the implementation of UN supported sustainable development and integration programs with nation states and big cities. Beyond this, they should elaborate models for efficient public service and conduct advisory and administrative activities. They should also promote and inspect UNBPM reimbursement and UN tax procedures, tenders, and effective utilization of convergence funds. They should create case studies and yearly reports. They should educate and qualify national public service officers. The centers could be the UN primary interface in any sub-regional affair. With all the above mentioned they could encourage nation states' cooperation and integration promoting their governance to join into a state union.

A **UN Joint Regional Center (UNJRC)** or a **UN Joint Country Center (UNJCC)** should be established on continents or in every large country comparable with them.

The centers should coordinate the planning and the implementation of UN supported sustainable development and integration programs and peace operations. All the activity was mentioned in relationship with UNSJC, they conduct on regional or large country level. The centers could be the UN primary interface in any regional or large country affair. In case of a developed region the center inspires state unions' or large countries' governance to generate different convergence funds and coordinates their utilization with the UN organizations. With the entire aforementioned task system they could encourage nation states' and sub-regions' cooperation and integration.

THE HIERARCHY OF THE UN JOINT CENTERS
(THEORETICAL VERSION)

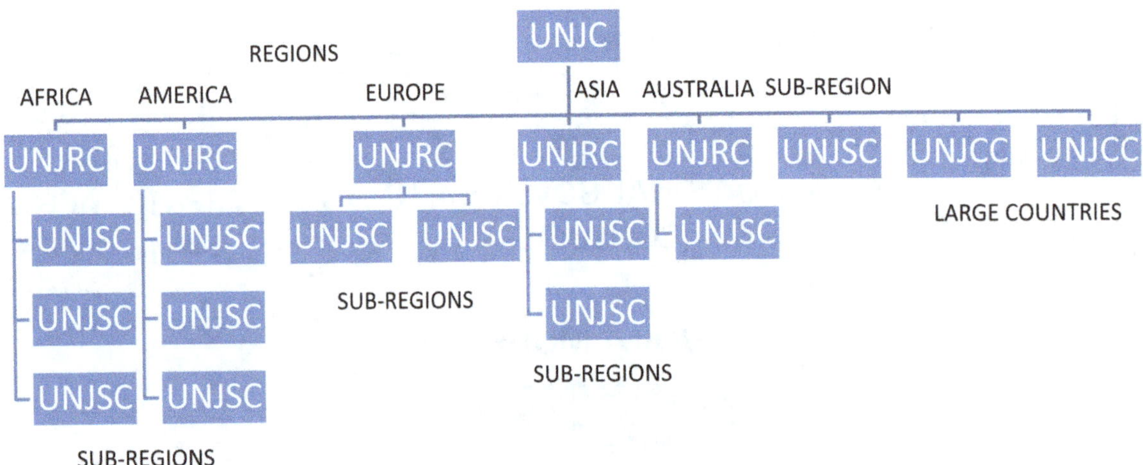

The current UN Center should be restructured into a **UN Joint Center (UNJC)**.

The UNJC should coordinate the activities of the UNJRCs and the UN non-joint organizations.

Presumably, during the global integration process, not every state in a sub-region intends to be a member of a state union for a short or long time.

Therefore, it is supposed to be a possibility when a UNJSC will be under direct coordination of the UNJC. Beyond this, the UNJC should cooperate with those standalone sustainable countries' governments, which are not willing to cooperate with any other joint centers.

In some strategic planning cycles, as a result of the gradually strengthening integration process, hopefully a **Global Union** could be established.

At the UNJC the **UN Assembly and the UN Security Council (UNSC)** is the main decision-making body. The UNSC decides on every affair related to introduction of any sanction against a government.

The **Peace and Stability Council,** together **with the other new councils,** are the main coordinating and decision-preparing bodies. In a reasonable time frame determined by the management they will be trying to reach a consensus and based on the result preparing a resolution to the UN Assembly or the UNSC for acceptance.

If a consensus is not reached they inform the **Management** and ask the **UN Secretary General** for assistance. If his or her actions were also not effective, councils deliver the issue to the UN Assembly or the UNSC to negotiate immediately.

The UN Secretary General should report yearly and publicly to the UN Assembly about the UN work accomplished under his or her direct coordination. The report should be accepted by the UN Assembly.

At UNJRC, UNJSC and UNJCC level there is no need to establish an assembly or a security council, because they should not be authorized to decide on any sanction- related issue and the parliament of a state or state union can substitute the UN Assembly.

If a consensus reached on an issue, a resolution suggestion should be submitted to the respective parliament. If the councilors of UNJSCs or UNJCCs could not reach consensus with their bodies they should send the affairs to the head of the UNJRC or the Secretary General together with a case report. Councilors of UNJSCs and UNJRCs and UNJCCs are authorized to send affairs directly to the UN Secretary General as well, if they judged an issue to be arranged urgently. The head of a UNJRC or a UNJCC should report to the parliament of a state union or a large country yearly and publicly about the UN work accomplished under his or her coordination. The report should be accepted by the respective parliament.

The **Financial Support Center** and the **Legal Support Center** of the joint centers should assume responsibility for the budget planning, tax collection and legal representation. Beyond this, they support the new councils and the management in the planning coordination of sustainable development and integration programs and their implementation.

THE COMPOSITION OF THE UN JOINT CENTERS
(THEORETICAL VERSION)

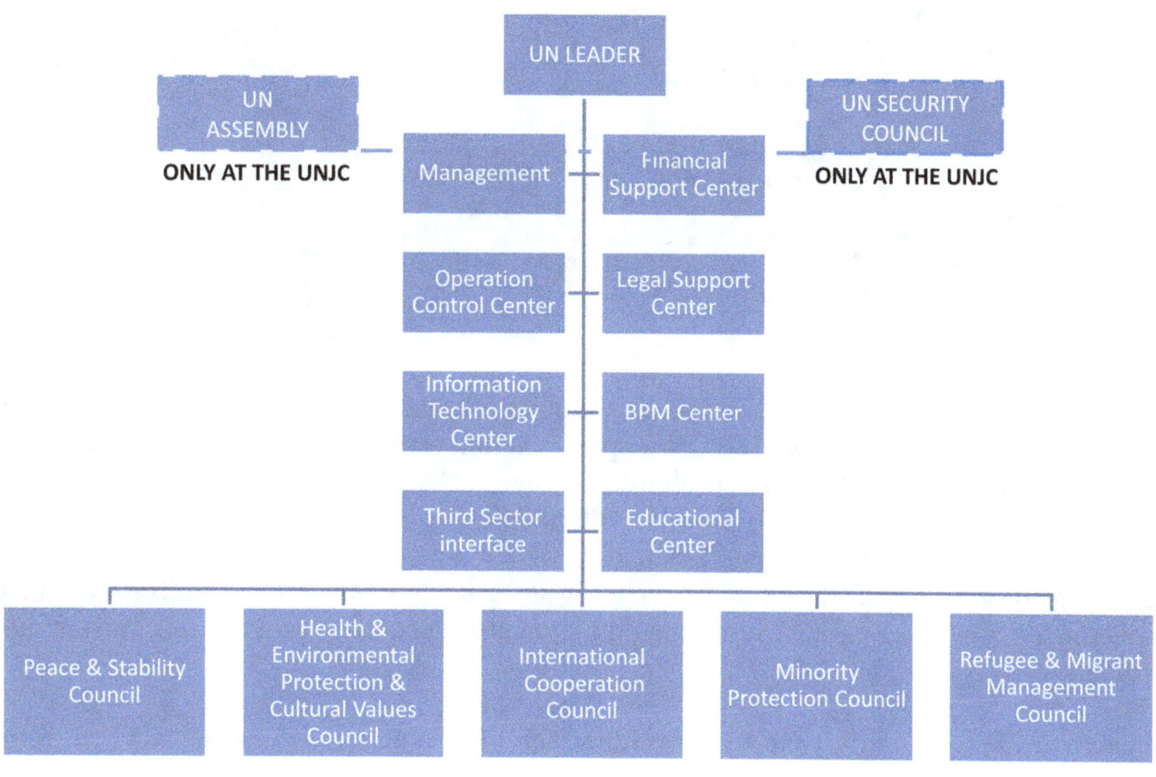

The UN staff members' assignment to the UN joint centers should be composed in accordance with their geographical location in the broadest spectrum. The position of nation states in the sustainable development and integration ranking list could be considered as well. The staff composition of joint centers may vary too, depending on their actual necessities. However, because of the transparency of the governance and especially the UN voting system the **UN Security Council's permanent members should share staff posts in equal portions in the Management and in the Information Technology Center.**

The UN joint centers should be modernized according to the information society's requirements. They should be provided with reliable hardware and software technology enabling UNBPM members to vote if requested. The structure of the UN joint centers may consist of a temporary mobile functional module with logistic, infrastructural and staff protection, telecommunication and helipad elements additionally in case of a more complex environment.

The establishment of the UN military and police command structure could be considered.

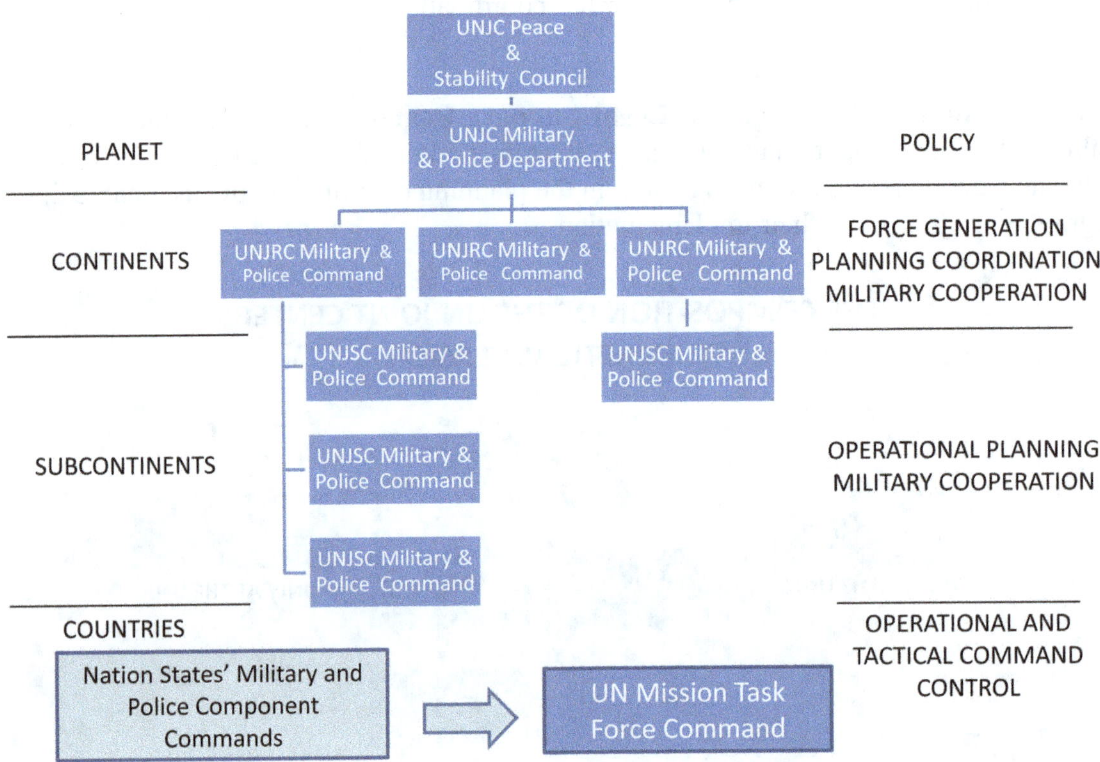

In order to guarantee that the UN can protect nations and ethnic groups from external attack, at least **a brigade size (about 6,000 people) UN rapid reaction military and police force** should be established shortly with expeditionary capabilities similar to NATO and the EU. Later on, **it should be increased to a corps size capability (about 50,000 people).**

The existence of joint UN centers could have a big influence on **non-joint organizations;** therefore the modernization of these organizations should be planned depending on the decision was made on joint centers.

For supporting the restructuring, the **UN should launch "UN blue bonds",** which could be paid back from the UN tax later.

5. Theoretical base for modernization (in a new UN Charter)

The majority of social conflicts originate from the mistreatment of minorities' real or believed grievances. The unmanaged minority affairs could lead to terrorism or war. That is why minority issues should be managed in a distinguished manner.

The reasons of disintegration should be examined thoroughly. Even though the aim of the global governance is the full integration of equal citizens, states and state unions are encouraged to support the minorities' freedom of self-determination.

If minorities comply with UN sustainable development principles and wish cultural or territorial autonomy their wish needs to be granted. The implementation should be linked to a gradual qualifying and controlling process elaborated by the UN experts.

If a nation state is not able to control the process peacefully, the minority should be placed under trusteeship of the UN and the possible escalation of the conflict needs to be examined and prevented.

Nation states and state unions are correct if they refrain from any projection of people's problems to their entire ethnical and cultural or religious identity.

Everyone needs to help refugees, who abandoned their home either by force or in the absence of humane living conditions. It is highly appreciated if refugees are provided with every conditions of normal life for example settlement, work and education. Nevertheless, the nation states and state unions have the right to register and contain illegally relocating people. They also have right to separate refugees from migrants, who left their home with hope of a better life. Every nation state or state union has the right to limit the number of received migrants.

Every state or state union has the right to self-defense; however this excludes any preventive or offensive action in out of home areas without a UN mandate. Nation states and state unions should respect territorial integrity and sovereignty of other states and respect the ownership of objects in international areas on Earth or in outer space. They are not authorized to monopolize or blockade any territory or object until their authority or ownership is discussed. The disputes relating to authority and the access of natural or man-made resources and line of communications should be arranged by negotiation. It is not allowed to endanger or ruin the biosphere and world heritage sites intentionally. It is forbidden to manipulate or to hack any voting or election organized by a country's government or the UN. Whoever violates these regulations should directly face the UN military or police forces' or an international military or police force's reaction by UN mandate. The original situation should be restored and the offender should be brought to the International Court of Justice.

6. The UN Security Council's composition and decision-making

6.1. Composition

For the supplement of the council the UN Assembly should nominate new permanent members for the UNSC. After the supplement the composition of the UNSC should provide a better geographical representation of continents and large countries equal to current and future state unions' regional power. Every member should get one mandate, but lead nations in a state union could divide their mandate, if they are willing. The UN should get a mandate for the representation of those people who cannot or do not want to join any nation state or state union. The UN Assembly should nominate additional temporary members in order to represent sub-regions and unrepresented nation states. The 2/3 majority voting possibility should be calculated.

6.2. Decision-making on security issues

The UNSC should decide when a sanction is at stake. Before a sanction is introduced a feasibility study and an impact assessment should be conducted. If a force should be deployed the willingness of states for peace enforcement and peace building operations should be accounted. The decision is valid if the resolution is supported by at least the 2/3 of majority, including all permanent members' affirmative support. If the vote did not reach the 2/3 majority a new resolution should be elaborated. If the 2/3 majority is reached but there is at least one permanent member, who does not support, the UN Secretary General is authorized to request the **Two Star Level UNBPM members' decisive vote.**

After the decision was made, a UN campaign on the Internet should be launched. Next, a computer program should select a "Jury Court" from the voters at random. **The Jury Court is adapted from ancient Athenian democracy, the institute of "Heliaia".[8]** The computer should select the court members depending on their broad geographical representation and the ranking list in sustainable development and integration competition. The nation states that are in the upper part of the table should get proportionally better representation. Beyond this, the voters' selection could be complied with gender and race equality principles. The Jury Court should decide on affairs by a simple majority. The decision's consequences should be obligatory for every nation state. Parties are authorized to report an appeal having suspended effects for a short time, on the basis that the computer system was hacked. If the accusing party was not able to prove that the system had been hacked, the vote is valid. If the hacking was proved, depending on the urgency, the UN Secretary General should consider whether he or she will ignore the appeal and validate the UN mandate, by **"Force majeure"** or not[9]. If the Secretary General ignored the appeal he or she should offer the resignation, because the neutrality rule was injured. The acceptance should be judged by those whose interest was injured.

If the case is deemed as not urgent, the Secretary General should request remedy actions for the correction of the computer system and the repeated vote.

DECISION - MAKING ON SECURITY ISSUES

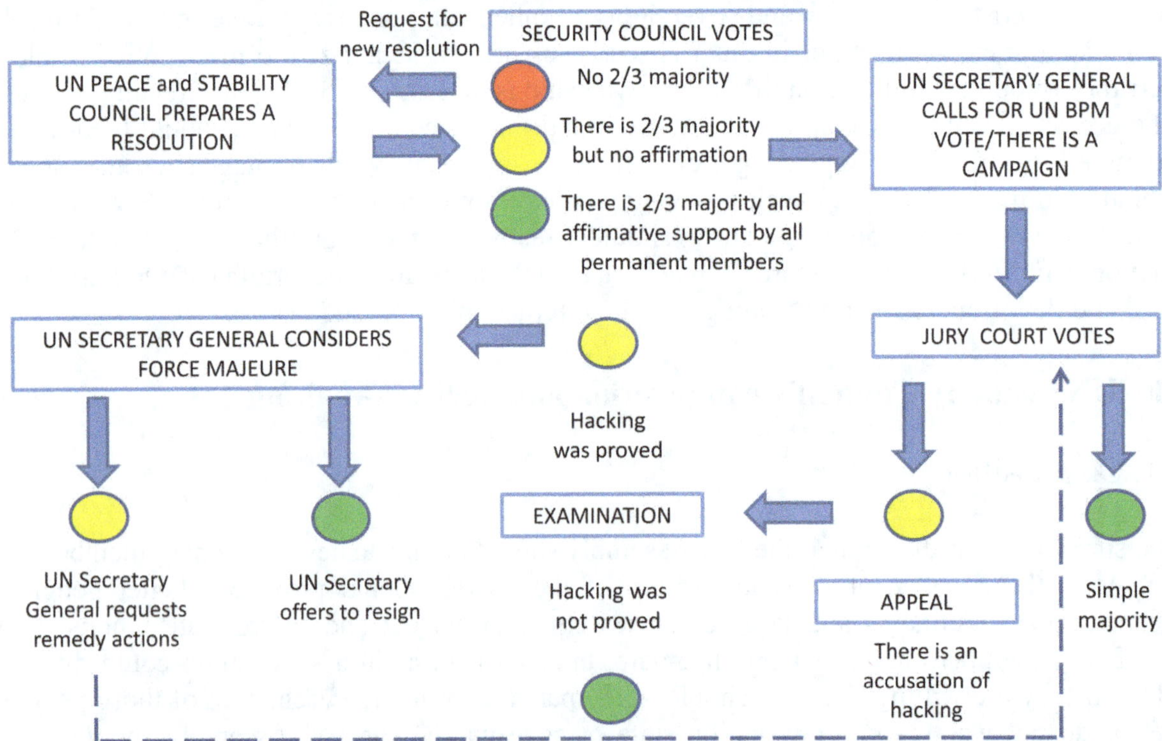

Some technical issues: The campaign materials should be simplified to "yes" or "no" or "A" or "B" questions finally (For example: Do you support a party, "yes" or "no"? Which party do you

---

8 Ηλιαία, Hliaea, was the Athenian supreme Court. The name derived from Ηλιαζεσθαι, gathering under the sun. The judges were named Heliasts, Ηλιασται, and there were 6,000 of them. Six hundred from each of the ten tribes. They were chosen by lot. It started judging all civil and penal cases, later also judged international disputes. In Quora, Internet, https://www.quora.com/What-exactly-was-the-function-of-the-Heliaia-in-Ancient-Athens
9 In the case of the Heliaia, if the vote was a draw, the president of Heliaia decided on behalf of Gods of Athens for the favor of the accused party.

support "A" or "B"?). The computer program could register potential Jury Court members who had met the voting requirements and submitted the voting intention in advance. After the registration time expired and some seconds before the vote, the computer program could deposit certain number of court members[10] as a voting deposit and a voting reserve randomly. A "time stamp" could be given on every selected member.

Then, a voting time window could be opened and every registered people could be requested to vote. Later, the computer program could close the voting time window and could search for the earlier selected court members' vote.

If the program could not find some votes, it could continue searching in the voting reserve and substitute the necessary number of votes from it.

Then the result could be summarized and shown.

In case of a hacking accusation, any person could be asked to answer: whether he or she voted with "yes" or "no" or "A" or "B". From the voluntary answers the accusation could be proved or refused easily.

Every Two Star Level UNBPM members could vote and the computer program could select the limited number[11] (60,001) of decisive votes randomly. So, any attempt to influence on the selected people's opinion would be very difficult, because the influence had to be directed to all UNBPM members. It would be spectacular and easily noticeable.

The official campaign materials could be uploaded to the UN website under UNSC's control.

The demonstrated solution could be working based on the sample of votes of the qualified outer majority. Those nations, which are in the upper part of sustainability and integration ranking list could have bigger representation. This way **the traditional force-based power components could be balanced with the new power components.** In other words: people in a less strong or smaller country could get relatively bigger representation in voting if their government is proceeding well in the sustainability and integration competition.

If a government would like to use any positive discrimination, it could be validated inside of a national voting sub-system. For example: if a government aware of that a minority has relatively small number of UNBPM members and the government would like that the votes of the minority were represented proportionally, then it is allowed for the government to ask the UN for setting up a proportional selection methodology in the national voting sub-system. The gender and race equality requirements could be set up depending on the relevant international accords.

In the case of the introduction of the adapted Heliaia type decision-making system in the UN, applying and validating the possibilities of future power components, it can be stated that the ancient democracy awakened a new generation level.

7. Strategic planning system

The Sustainable Development and Integration Planning System (SDIPS) adapted from NATO and the EU planning systems. The planning events could be rolling on in a two year cycle. The relevant planning period is ten years. The first year contains a highly detailed program structure with resources, the second and third years are still detailed, and the remaining years are less detailed. Every planning document should be composed on the functional construction of subject areas shown in the chapter 3. It is important, that every organization's formal output should be a formal input of another's. The issues with minor importance may have results in the system every two years and the issues of

---

10 Taking into account the number of UN member countries (193) and the simple majority rule, the concept suggests 60,001 court members to be selected, plus a reserve. This way, the average number of court members from a country could be about 310 people. It could be increased or reduced depending on the result of a government in sustainability and integration competition.

11 Even though the information technology could allow accounting all the votes, the voting system intentionally limits the number of voting people. The limitation intends to qualify the votes in favor of those countries whose government has a better performance in the sustainability and integration competition. It could be a tool for the UN to motivate governments in reaching good results.

strategic importance can be validated every ten years at the least.

Based on a **scrutiny** the planning should be initiated by **"Secretary General's Guidance"** (it may conclude the sustainable development and integration principles and the directions in evaluation methodology, shown in the chapter 2.2.).

After that, based on a **resource estimate,** the UNJC should elaborate the **sustainable development and integration goals and program suggestions** to the coordinated UNJRCs and those governments (partners), which directly cooperate with the UNJC. The **UNJRCs should clarify** the suggestions for their coordinated UNJSCs and cooperating partners. The **UNJSCs similarly and gradually clarify** the suggestions for their partners.

Based upon their resource estimate and goals, **partners should plan which UN goal and program they will accept, partially accept, consider or not accept.**

Next, the joint centers should plan their convergence programs proportionally depending on how the partners plan their contribution.

As the planning year turns into a new one, based on the **budget calculation,** the **UN joint centers should refine their goals and programs**. The partners do the same and they fill out the **"Sustainable Development and Integration Planning Questionnaire" (SDIPQ)**. Beyond the planned data, the SDIPQ should consist of the reports about the earlier program implementations. Based on that and their case control reports, the UN joint centers will analyze and negotiate the reported data with partners. They should get an **evaluation,** which goes into their record, **"Government Chapter"**. Until a state union represented its states in planning, its members fill out a questionnaire separately. **Based on the aggregation the UNJC should issue a new sustainable development and integration ranking list.**

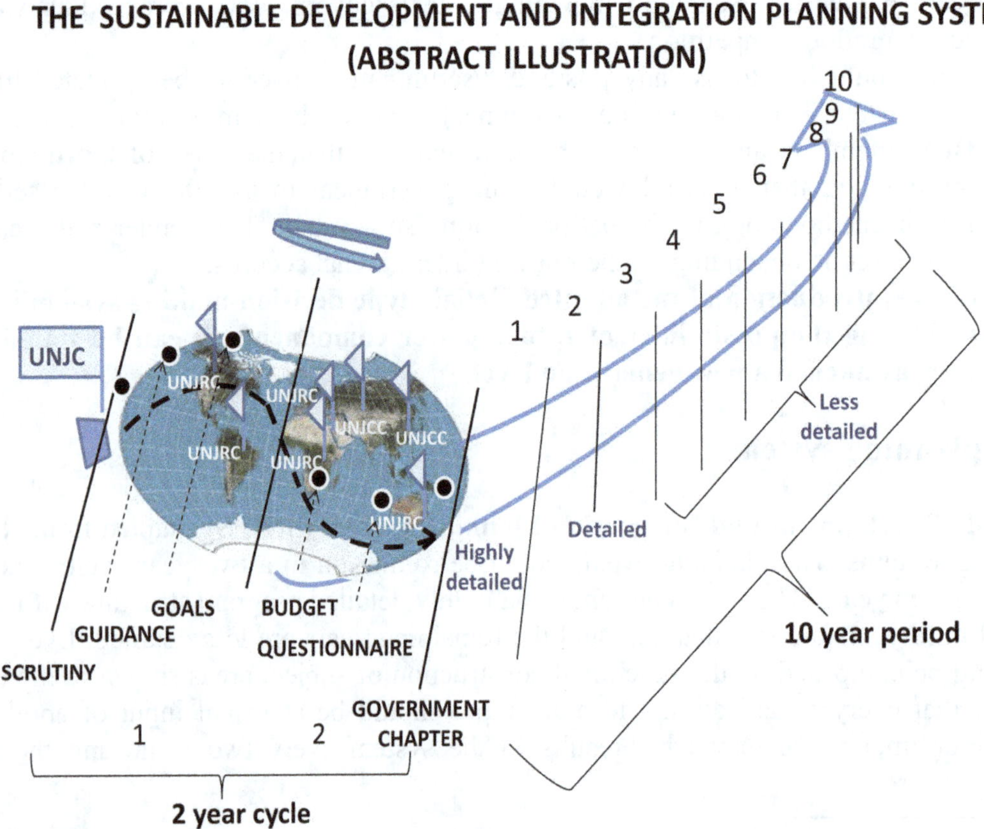

The budget contributions could be collected according to the Sustainable Development and Integration Ranking List (SDIRL) proportionally.

In accordance with the SDIRL, the membership of UN Security Council's permanent members could be reaffirmed or shifted. The UN Assemble could authorize the selection of the lead nation(s) in every geographical region.

This way the composition of the council could follow the changes of world power structure in the future. This makes sure there will not be a contradiction of interest in decision-making between ruling powers and real world power structure. So, it does not make sense to veto frequently or initiate an armed apocalypse.

8. Suggestions for the implementation

In the planning period an **Operative Planning and Control Group (OPCG)** should be designated and it should elaborate a detailed Master Plan.

In accordance with the UN Secretary General sustainable development and integration goals the OPCG should initiate and coordinate the elaboration of the **experimental unified evaluation system of the sustainable development and integration and the modified UN Charter.** In accordance with the promised host nation support new organizations (the new joint centers) and their location should be planned.

A Financial plan should be elaborated.

In the preparation period the UN should launch the **Blue Bonds. Consensus should be reached** on the experimental evaluation system and the modified UN Charter **with UNSC's permanent member states. Tenders** for joint centers' infrastructure should be opened.

In the third period the establishment of the new organizations should be accomplished in two phases:

Phase A:
    I. The UNJC (it should be located in a neutral country or in international territory)
    II. By the UNJC coordinated organizations (UNJRCs, UNJCCs, and standalone UNJSCs).
When they are ready for work, the experimental Sustainable Development and Integration System (SDIPS), the experimental UN tax system, a brigade size military and police quick reaction force, the One Star Level UNBPM system should be operated.

Phase B:
    III. By the UNJRC coordinated organizations and the non-joint organizations.
When they are ready for work, the SDIPS, the UN tax system, a corps sized military and police quick reaction force, the Two Star Level UNBPM system and the new decision-making system should be operated. Based on the preliminary calculation, the estimated time for the entire implementation could be planned for a ten year long period.

How to overcome the difficulties?

The suggested model may go against corporate and business lobby groups' interest and it may conflict with natural inner resistance of the UN bureaucratic institutions.

Therefore, it is conceivable that representatives of the UN will not be able to coordinate the above demonstrated profound changes. **The accomplishment requires intergovernmental agreements, which need to be coordinated by one of the permanent member states of the UN Security Council.**

"Solutions are not easy to come by. Changing the power structure of the Security Council is no easy matter, with the permanent members unwilling to give up their position of advantage."[12]

Yes. There will be difficulties in creating an effective world power for Security Council's, permanent members as well, because the mutual trust of permanent members wavered when some of them conducted an armed intervention or other type of expansion in the absence of consensus. For example: China's opinion was neglected before the Korean War and Russia's as well during the Yugoslavian Crisis and the Iraqi War.

The events on the Crimean Peninsula and Donetsk area and on the South China Sea could irritate Britain, France and the United States, who could be hurt otherwise too, because her earlier attempts as a champion of democracy were not acknowledged on the level which she deserved.

Nevertheless, each of the current permanent members could be able to take advantage of the

---

12 Ronald Niezen: Is the United Nations broken? In: Sapiens 01 Nov 2017, Internet,
https://www.sapiens.org/culture/united-nations-broken/

opportunity and could be leader of changes. Britain could utilize her transatlantic mediator role. China could capitalize her development, which she gained in trading cooperation. France could exploit her momentum, which she has got in the modernization of society and excellent peace building process with a former adversary. Russia could reach one of her permanent objectives in security policy to raise up the UN flag onto a higher level. The United States, with her financial restrictions and withdrawal from some of the UN projects, may enforce real structural changes to the UN.

The European Union (EU) as an example of a great modernization attempt could be able to lead the changes as well and she could build social cohesion of her member states further and could really reach the wished role as a global player.

The current permanent members and regional, sub-regional alliances and large sustainable countries could put together their efforts and lead or join the social revolution in international affairs.

They could break down newly emerging WMD powers and bring up people from poverty. They could build a common UN house from people's personal initiations to protect their environment. Emphasizing environmental protection targets, people could support that UN bonds were issued and a corporate tax management was developed.

They could exclude the unfair attempts made by different lobby groups to influence impartial decision-making. They could transform existing regional UN institutions and they could increase their numbers in developing areas.

In order to reduce confrontations with the UN staff members, the Joint UN Center and joint regional and sub- regional centers and country centers could be established at the beginning. Their post biddings could be opened for those experts, who work for different non-joint organizations as well, such as the specialized agencies, departments and offices. The UN non-joint organizations' duplications could be removed after that the new organizations reached their operational readiness.

The technological revolution is already ongoing. It needs to be accelerated by establishing favorable social circumstances.

As a result of the synergy of structural changes in the UN, a new progressive international regulation system in international affairs could be composed and world governance could be operated effectively.

The UN Security Council's member states are requested to allow the outer qualified majority of people decided in every conflict, in which the traditional decision-making had stuck earlier.

Everyone is invited to assemble under a more brightly shining blue UN flag!

Summary

Global challenges could be managed by effective world governance, which promote sustainability and integration in human development.

There is no time and alternative to risk the establishment of new world governance after a devastating war. Therefore, the existing intergovernmental organization, the United Nations must be reformed.

The GDP as a measurement of human development should be improved to a direction where sustainability and the level of integration are preferred.

There is a suggestion in this essay to express a kind of new sustainable GDP (SGDP). Based on SGDP, relative values of different subject areas could be expressed. With using multipliers (coefficients), the level of integration also could be preferred, depending on the level of sub-regional, regional, or global cooperation.

This way, relative values could be unified as well. Based on the new evaluation system, a sustainable development and integration ranking list of governments could be composed.

Based on the ranking list, a new voting system in the UN could be operated. The decision-making system on security issues should be supplemented with new legal institutions of Jury Court and Force majeure. Jury Court' decision on security issues could be based on the UN Blue Planet Movement's (UNBPM) members' vote on the Internet. Conscientious UNBPM members, who are out of the area of a problem, could represent not only their own interest but the other people's too. A computer system could select Jury Court members randomly; therefore Jury Court's decision could be a sample of an outer qualified majority of people.

The UN functional structure could be composed depending on interdependent global challenges and sustainable development and integration goals accordingly.

The hierarchical structure could be more effective with establishing joint UN center, joint sub-regional and regional centers, and joint country centers. The UN Security Council's membership could be supplemented and shifted according to geographical requirements and the changing world power structure. The UN Charter should be modernized. A new coordinated Sustainable Development and Integration Planning System could be introduced.

The proactive crisis management capability of the UN must be developed. The UN self-sustainability must be established.

It may be difficult for world leaders to agree with the accomplishment of such a reform. Nevertheless, it would be easier to accept it than to win a third world war or to reverse deadly environmental changes.

The representatives of a qualified majority and their children, grandchildren and people who are not yet born cry out for survival and request clear regulation of fair and useful competition in human development, instead of narrow-minded political games and a ruined environment.

Sources

Annual and quarterly reports on global risks: Global Catastrophic risks 2016-2018, published by Global Challenges Foundation, Internet, https://globalchallenges.org/en/our-work/annual-report

United Nations: Funds, Programs, Specialized Agencies and Others, Internet, http://www.un.org/en/sections/about-un/funds-programmes-specialized-agencies-and-others/

United Nations: UN Charter. Internet, http://www.un.org/en/sections/un-charter/un-charter-full-text/

Transforming our world: the 2030 Agenda for Sustainable Development. Sustainable Development Goals, Knowledge Platform, Internet, https://sustainabledevelopment.un.org/post2015/transformingourworld

Mark Malloch-Brown: The UN is an under-funded, bureaucratic labyrinth - and a force for good in the world. In: The Telegraph 26 Jun 2015, Internet, https://www.telegraph.co.uk/news/worldnews/11699243/The-UN-is-an-under-funded-bureaucratic-labyrinth-and-a-force-for-good-in-the-world.html

Franz Baumann: UN bureaucracy? No, Thanks. In: Pass Blue Independent Coverage of the UN. 14 May 2016, Internet, https://www.passblue.com/2016/05/14/un-bureaucracy-no-thanks/

President Trump says bureaucracy is stopping UN from reaching its full potential in debut appearance. In: UN, South China Morning Posts, Edition Hong Kong.
19 September 2017, Internet, https://www.scmp.com/news/world/united-states-canada/article/2111743/president-trump-says-bureaucracy-and-mismanagement

Ronald Niezen: Is the United Nations broken? In: Sapiens 01 Nov 2017. Internet, https://www.sapiens.org/culture/united-nations-broken/

Norms and Standards for Evaluation. UN Evaluation Group. New York 2017, Internet, http://www.unevaluation.org/document/detail/1914

Tadanori Inomata: Strategic Planning in the United Nations System. Joint Inspection Unit. Geneva 2012. Internet,
https://www.unjiu.org/sites/www.unjiu.org/files/jiu_document_files/products/en/reports-notes/JIU%20Products/JIU_REP_2012_12_English.pdf
Greek Law. In: Encyclopedia Britannica. Internet, https://www.britannica.com/topic/Greek-law

Top 3 methods for measuring economic development. In: Economics Discussion network. Internet,
http://www.economicsdiscussion.net/economics-2/top-3-methods-for-measuring-economic-development/4423

The future of minorities in the globalized world. Publications of the United Nations Associations of Hungary. Hungarian, edited by Erwin Gömbös, Budapest, 2016. ISBN 978-963-89728-1-1

Attachment: The results of theoretical modeling

The model was checked theoretically based on the following criteria: core values, decision-making capacity, effectiveness, resources and financing, trust and insight, flexibility, protection against the abuse of power, accountability.

1. Core values

Based on the human goodness, the UN Blue Planet Movement (UNBPM) enables people to contribute to environmental protection personally. Supposedly, the UNBPM would be a step forward in the development of democratic institutions and information society. With the acceptance of UNBPM principles everybody could be a UNBPM member. The UNBPM centers could be connected to the UN Information Technology Center in which public information and vote accounting systems operate. This way people could be informed about UN decision-making, thus they could be a part of it. Everybody could express his or her opinion regularly. People, who agree with UN principles, proving a clean life record, taking a basic test on the Internet, and an oath, could be authorized to participate in a decisive vote. The model calls for a better geographical representation in the UN Security Council and provides possibility for representation of those people who cannot or do not want to connect to any nation state in the future. "Ordinary" people in Jury Court could decide on questions, in which UN decision-making system was paralyzed earlier. According to the member states' position in the sustainable development ranking list, the computer system could select voting people based on the race and gender equality principles.

Older people play an important social role in various cultures. In the interest of professional governance, people welcome rich business men, who have enough life and social experience and usually do not involve any corruption. People think their personal success is a guarantee of state's prosperity.

The UN Councilors in the model could comply with requirements of impartiality. During their working activity they would not make any sanction-related decisions. Therefore, they could assume important responsibility at the top of UN future joint centers as a guardian and facilitator of human rights and justice, peace and social development. The model takes account of supporters' goodness and their sense of responsibility.

2. Decision-making capacity

Governmental steps could be comparable with the UN standards applied for the evaluation system of sustainable development. Decision-makers could more objectively judge on possible sanctions.

With the enhancement of the UN regional institutions the UN subject matter experts could have a closer working relationship with national experts. As a result, they could recognize and analyze a potential crisis source more effectively. Beyond this, they could take remedy actions locally.

Councilors could be authorized to report any urgent issue directly to the Secretary General. Especially, the sanction-related reports could run forward with high priority. In accordance with the structure of the functional subject areas; coordinated bodies' formal outputs are inputs of the coordinating bodies in the Sustainable Development and Integration Planning System. This way the reporting system could be operated with a reasonable burden sharing for role-players. It could accelerate the reporting process. The nation states' petitions and UN case studies made by staff workers could reach the top level at the same time. Therefore, preparatory actions could be taken quickly. The top level organization could only request a possible supplement. This could reduce the time of examination and preparation of a decision. Regional joint centers could share the burdens on crisis management issues and free up capacities at the top. The higher level organizations could oversee their priorities quickly. This way the decision-making capacity would not be shrunk, thus new effective possibilities could be open. The support of decisions by people could be measured by UNBPM members' votes, which strengthens the credibility of the chosen course of actions.

All of the UN democratic institutions could be matched to one of the ancient Athenian democratic institutions, except one, the "Heliaia", which was a Jury Court. The Jury Court and UN Secretary General's "Force majeure" could bring a solution in a case when the conventional part of decision-making is paralyzed. This way the decision-making capacity could be increased. The extended decision-making capacity allows the supplement of the UN Security Council; otherwise the decision-making would be even more problematic.

3. Effectiveness

The source providers (the UN experts) of different subjects in the Joint UN centers and the consumers (the national experts) are in one place at the same time during their cooperation. Their work could be more efficient than in the fragmented structure.

After mutual evaluation of the UN joint organizations' and consumers' experts, consensus could be reached and a consolidated Government Chapter elaborated. If a government does not comply with the requirements, there would be a final sanctioning instrument. If the repeated warning of UN top level organizations was not effective the convergence funds could be reduced or suspended until the amendments were taken. The consumers' efforts could be acknowledged in the sustainable development and integration ranking list regularly. Presumably, governments would be interested in reaching a better result, because it would increase their prestige.

With the integration of connecting governance functions and planning coordination the model strives to comply with the increasing global challenges. The world governance's reaction capabilities could be more effective with the new regional joint centers. The UN could have a better chance to coordinate state unions' and nation states' contributions to raise up developing regions.

The rolling planning system could be a guarantee of the effective implementation. The whole UN structure and work could be scrutinized periodically against the global challenges and risks. In order to meet the new requirements, the necessary actions could be taken.

Nowadays, there are more conflicts, which lack the perfect consensus of the UN Security Council's permanent members, but have been solved by force. Instead of moving further into this direction, permanent members could be requested to start a new beginning. That is why the model suggests the modernization of the UN principles in the UN Charter.

The model suggests a complex decision-making system for effective implementation of sanction-related decisions, which could be based on the UN Security Council's permanent members' conventional power and Jury Court's decision. The first traditionally could enforce, the second alternatively inspire the implementation. The Jury Court's decision would express people's support, which could be inspiring; taking into account that the value of the people's supported decisions are more precious and long-lasting than any enforcement. The permanent members' affirmative support requirement in the UN Security Council decision-making is obviously intended to prevent large scale conflicts; however, sometimes exactly this requirement prevented the intervention from being in time. Sometimes, ethnic groups and small nations could be victim on the big powers' strategic chess play.

The future of the UN is highly dependent on how it would be able to get out of this contradiction. If permanent members would not accept the suggestion in the model, at least they should accept it partially in the beginning, to those cases when they are directly not involved in a conflict. This way the model would prevent a large scale escalation and the ethnic groups and small nations could be protected better.

In order to guarantee that the UN can protect nations and ethnic groups from external attack, the model suggests the establishment of the UN rapid reaction military and police force.

The new impartial UN leaders, the UN Councilors could mediate in crisis management and provide assistance in handling internal disputes fairly. The model could allow and expect a more proactive crisis management for the UN and that is why a permanent trusteeship representation could be established in the management of joint centers.

According to the character of global challenges the model could provide effective possibilities for planning coordination, monitoring and evaluation.

Furthermore, it could inspire governments for effective resource consumption, which together with the increasing decision-making capacity could ensure the effective implementation of decisions.

4. Resources and financing

The UNBPM reimbursements could be financed with people's contributions and companies' promotions. By shopping and using environmentally friendly products, people could save energy. From their savings they could be able to shop for more products and this could result in a bigger profit for the interested companies and banks. This could increase the quantity of products on the market and as a result, the price could be lowered. Companies and banks could have a better possibility for innovation and UN support. The UN could invite companies to tender for technology modernization. Company owners could support convergence funds from their extra income. Multilevel supporters could be leaders, the UN Councilors of the joint UN centers. It could be a positive prosperity chain mechanism. Companies and banks would be requested to pay a small part of their corporate tax to UN. Supposedly, governments' leaders and companies' owners and managers could understand that it would be more favorable and of course cheaper for them than financing the direct costs of operations against world global challenges. If there is no peace and stability in developing regions then there will not be enough resources for environmental and health protection; cultural values could be pushed to the background. These could result in a mass of relocating and conflicting people with diseases and a ruined environment. In the lack of cooperation and minority protection there could be more terrorist activities and armed conflicts. The developed regions would be enforced to spend a lot to reconcile them. The result could be more efficient if the crisis management is more proactive.

The UN joint centers' coordinating efforts with the assistance of the new planning system could contribute to the efficiency of resource consumption. In contrast with the fragmented structure, joint centers could provide a more cost effective operation; because the concentrated functional elements could be operated by less service support and their duplication could be ignored. The staff's travel necessities could also be reduced.

The UN restructuring could be supported by "UN blue bonds". Bonds could be paid back from UN tax later. This way the UN could be more independent from available wavering national contributions. After restructuring, the possible reduced operating cost of non-joint elements may lead to a more effective operation. The UN member states could contribute to the UN budget based on their position in the sustainable development ranking list proportionally.

Staff posts could be filled based on the former approach (geographical distribution, performance, morality, gender equity) and according to the sustainable development and integration ranking list. Hopefully, it would not conflict with the targeted distribution principles. The new joint regional and sub-regional centers could provide a fair chance to comply with geographical distribution requirements. Their posts could be filled in mainly from their regions and sub-regions. Nevertheless, wherever it is possible, distribution by the sustainable development ranking list could compromise with source providers' in their contribution.

Having a better knowledge of the circumstances, joint centers' staff could be a problem sensitive membrane of the global governance. The model could provide sufficient human and material resources, and that these resources could be financed in an equitable manner.

5. Trust and insight

Evaluation standards give potential for a more objective evaluation. The joint centers' hierarchy and their coordinating efforts could provide a closer working relationship with the representatives of regions and sub-regions. The UN Security Council's campaign materials on the Internet could provide people with an insight into UN decision-making. The UNBPM voting system and the institution of Jury Court and the UN Secretary General's resignation rule in case of Force majeure may strengthen people's trust in the UN decision-making.

The UN financial organizations' activity could be more understandable and friendly, because the joint centers' experts could decide on the conditions of the resource consumption with the state unions' and states' experts together.

The respected UN councilors would stand above all political and economic interest. They, together with their UN organizations' staff, could be interested in only the sustainability and integration. The UN Joint organizations' yearly reports sent well in advance to the UN Assembly or the parliament of the states and state unions, could provide potential to oversee all the UN work. Reports could be published and transmitted by the telecommunication assets and the questions and answers period could be followed by people online. Practically, the consumers (state unions' and states parliaments and even people) could monitor the world governance's work permanently. Expectedly, the model could provide good possibilities for gaining people's trust.

6. Flexibility

"Third sector interface" and the lesson learned organization in the managements of the joint centers could provide possibilities for the involvement of the UN staff and private researchers in restructuring. Monitoring and anti-corruption organization in managements could prepare and collect regular reports and case studies. Based on them, the UN Secretary General could consider any actions which should be taken. The model could provide the scrutiny of the structure every two years. The cyclic restructuring could be initiated by the UN Secretary General's Guidance for sustainable development accordingly. The major changes with strategic importance could be suggested at least every ten years. According to the suggested evaluation system, the UN budget contribution could be calculated in every two years. The Security Council's permanent members could also be replaced in every ten years. The changes in principles and evaluation could result in adjustments in the composition of sustainable development and integration programs and in the organizations' function. It could have influence on the structure. Peace operations' necessities could be reported to the operational center and further to planning coordinators and current operation mangers. This way, the urgent issues could be arranged and the structure related issues entered into the system. The planning of sustainable development and the peace operations' support could be connected into a harmonized system. In other words: if changes were needed in principle, the system could initiate changes in the structure and the peace operation support automatically. Thereby, the system makes sure that the UN structure and the peace operations' support could be pushed to the direction of the development of world global challenges.

7. Protection against the abuse of power

The monitoring, the anti-corruption, the complaints and the lesson learned organizations in the managements of the joint centers could operate a controlling subsystem, which could provide possibility to recognize any abuse of power. The staff composition requirement in the managements and in the information technology centers could reduce the possibility of abuse of power.

Money is power, therefore, the model would delineate the policy and the source provider functions in the structure. The joint centers' coordinating subject matter experts could determine the policy of the source consumption together with national experts. The UN financial organizations could be dealing with "only" the fund generation and financial techniques. The source provision process supposes the coordinated efforts of different experts on different planning events. Not a narrow group could decide on the consumption, but many people could be involved into it. This way the resource estimates, the budget plans and the payments could be controlled better.

The impartial UN Councilors could guarantee the UN joint centers' staff members do not overstep their mandate.

8. Accountability

Nation states could fill out the Sustainable Development and Integration Questionnaire in the final part of the planning cycle and this way they could prepare a formal report about changes in their plan and the improvements they reached in implementation.

A focused part of the report could deal with development programs and the provision of their resources. The UN joint centers' staff members could compare the report with their case studies and control results. Next, they could elaborate evaluations, in which government chapters could be negotiated by national experts.

In the case of a government not complying, sanctions could be introduced. Depending on how the available resources were utilized, the new resources could be provided fully, on a reduced level or suspended. If an accusation of corruption was proved, resources could be returned.

The monitoring and anti-corruption organizations in the management could control the inner resource consumption as well. The report could include the implementation of resource consumption and the reason of possible delays and their risks. The human resource organization in the managements could operate a human qualifying system, which could be built on national counter-parties' feedback. The complaints organization in the managements could be opened for direct reception of any petition from the bottom up to the highest level. The security organization in the managements could check whether the staff conflicts with UN interest or not. The property declaration could be part of the security check.